Reflections
not quite a memoir

DAMIAN GALBO

www.peppertreepublishing.com

Copyright © Damian Galbo, 2024

All rights reserved. Published by the Peppertree Press, LLC. The Peppertree Press and associated logos are trademarks of the Peppertree Press, LLC. No part of this publication may be reproduced, stored in a retrieval system, transmitted in any form or by any means, electronic, mechanical, photocopying, recording, or otherwise, without prior written permission of the publisher and author/illustrator. Graphic design by Elizabeth Parry.

For information regarding permission, call 941-922-2662 or contact us at our website: www.peppertreepublishing.com or write to: The Peppertree Press, LLC, Attention: Publisher, 715 N. Washington Blvd., Suite B, Sarasota, Florida 34236

ISBN: 978-1-61493-975-7
Library of Congress: 2024916465
Printed: October 2024

Manufactured in the United State of America

Other books by: Damian Galbo
Reaching Inward

Reflections:

A collection of poems and essays exploring topics current today and in the past. Some of the content is autobiographical and true. However, in all cases, names have been changed.

"Raise your words, not your voice.
It is Rain that grows flowers,
Not thunder."
Rumi-

Dedication

To my late Godmother, Agatha, and my close friend Jimmy.
Each of you has
saved me more times
than I can remember

Preface

It's difficult for me to believe that any author begins a book knowingly writing about himself. To me, that seems quite presumptuous thinking that anyone out there in the reading public would care two whits about the author's life.

But I believe what happens inevitably is that in writing about events which occurred in one's life, and about people one has met in the corridors of one's life, then what happens is that the words start to look closely like some kind of memoir.

Certainly, there are the requisite blogs and essays today called "opinion pieces." There could be a smattering of poetry, some episodes from the author's distant past, or maybe not so distant past. At some point it may begin to resemble a "memoir". Of course, most names are changed before putting them down on paper. But, dearest reader, allow me to warn you; try not to be fooled; authors can be very tricky.

I shall leave the labeling to you to determine if what you read qualifies to be called "a memoir." All I know is I had a blast putting all these words down on paper.

D. Galbo

Table of Contents

Time and Distance 1
Love 2
Alone in a Crowd 3
Trying to Discover 4
Connection 5
Eddie 7
West Virginia 11
Some Dental Ruminations
   The Menacing Cotton Roll 17
   Children 20
   The 99-Year-Old 23
   Lisa Marie 29
   Veronica 38
Change 41
Remnants 43
When 44
Sensations 46
Upstairs and Down - Measuring
   What Has Been Lost 47
Civilization's Demise 53
Some Sobering Thoughts 56
Thoughts on Life 60
Love 61
Letters to My Brother 62
   The Huge and Unrelenting Chasm
      in America 76
   It's All About Control 83
Love Lost 90
Mirage 92
Danger? 95
Maybe It Is Time 97
Raison d'être 99
My Wish for Myself 101

Time and Distance

   She reaches out her hand
         to touch me

   I had promised that I
         would always be there
               to take it

   But time and distance
         have conspired to render
               that impossible

   My tortured heart
         is about ready
               to explode

   I cannot imagine
         what she is feeling

Damian Galbo

Love

    Aching
    and shaking
    wanting to scream

    Is this what it's like
    with
    cocaine,
    heroin?

    You would think
    that at my age
    I would know
    these things

    If a lab took a sample
    of my saliva,
    my blood,
    my DNA

    Would their tests
    show anything

    about longing

    about love

    about you?

Alone in a Crowd

>Sitting here in a crowded room
>distilling my thoughts of you
>from the clamor
>
>Staring at the blank faces
>as they vie with you
>for my attention
>
>Doomed to fail
>
>Your face so clear
>your hair, your eyes
>your warmth
>I can nearly touch you
>
>It's crazy how alone we are
>amongst all these bodies

Damian Galbo

Trying to Discover

who I am,
not who I was,
is nearly impossible
these days

I am confused
like entropy
in a quantum wound

When I allow
the chaos
to settle
I can sometimes
barely discern
my own arms
outstretched

seeking

a home

Connection

A few years ago I was living in a different community here in Florida. On a small corner of the property was a tiny putting and chipping green. I would often bike over there in the early evening to practice and to soak up the ambiance of nature. I was almost always alone except for the little critters and the birds.

One evening, a small doe, about four feet high decided to pay me a visit and watch me putt and chip. It was a thrill to have her with me—she is certainly one of God's most perfect creatures.

On about the fourth day in a row she started to get more curious and began slowly walking toward me on the green. I am sure she was sensing no threat from me as she kept coming closer and closer, until she was but one yard away. I was full of adrenalin from the excitement and had to work hard to stay calm.

Dropping my golf club I slowly extended my hand. She looked at my open palm and after what seemed like a minute or two, but was actually only about fifteen seconds, she touched my hand with her tongue. Then she commenced licking my hand. I believe she needed the contact as much as I did then.

My little friend then raised up on her hind legs, put both her front legs on my chest, then rested her head right on me. I dared not breathe for fear of losing this moment. I wished there was someone near who could document that moment with a picture, but there was no one that I could see.

My new friend and I hugged like this for about a minute. Then she got down and walked very slowly away, never once taking her eyes off me.

When she was finally out of range, I dropped to my knees and thanked God for that moment of bliss.

Another miracle happened not quite a half hour later. A pedestrian approached me and told me that she had been near the woods and quietly saw the whole thing. She was very excited because she had taken a picture on her phone. My jubilation was off the charts.

That picture of the two of us embracing is on my closet wall and I see it every day and try to revisit those feelings. Sometimes I actually can.

NB: The picture is on the back cover of this book.

Eddie

As I think back on a long career in dentistry, I find it amazing just how close I came to being something or someone else. There seem to be two or three periods in each person's life when an extremely important decision is made influenced mainly by surrounding events.

This is as it was, as I was peacefully and happily seeking my chemistry degree from college. My applications for graduate schools were all in place and even some acceptances and fellowships were being offered. I seemed to have few cares in the world when I just happened to stop by a classmate's room to grab some food. Then everything changed.

Eddie Michaels lived next door to me in the dorm, but he was one of those rare birds one never saw. His parents lived only an hour from campus, so Fast Eddie was off every weekend to home to get some real chow. This particular Saturday I heard his stereo and knocked on his door.

"Yo, Fast Eddie."

"Blade, how's it goin', man?" (I need to digress a bit—my nickname was Blade, given to me early in my days growing up in Brooklyn. We'll leave the reasons for another time.)

"Good, Eddie. I heard your music and am surprised that you're still here this weekend. Was wondering if you have any of your mom's goodies left over? I've been getting all these acceptances to grad school and all this decision-making is making me hungry."

"Yeah, Blade, like you never used to grab food from me and my mom before all these decisions," he laughed, "Come on over and help yourself."

And so I did—homemade cookies, pound cake with chocolate icing—Nirvana. It's a wonder Eddie wasn't huge!

"So what are you doing here this weekend, Eddie?" I asked, as I noticed him carving some chalk thing.

"Well, the dental boards are coming up and I need to practice my carving so I can hopefully pass. Easier to do it here than at home with all those distractions," he said. "You see this little stick here? I have to somehow turn it into a tooth.

"Wow, Eddie, it actually looks a bit like a tooth already. I had no idea you were thinking about dental school. A dentist! Cripes, I haven't been to one in years. And I sure as hell wouldn't want to be one—always poking around in strange people's mouths, breathing in their germs. Gotta be awful—bad breath, screaming kids—whew!"

"Not so fast, Blademan! Remember last summer when you worked as a chemist at the National Laboratory? You did all the work on that research project?"

"Yeah, I remember."

"Well, who got the credit?"

"Yeah, the head of the department did and my name wasn't even on the paper. That was bad."

"And do you recall telling me something about your wanting a few days off and they refused?"

"Yes, come to think of it." I said. "That really was the pits. I lost out on a few days of fun and games with someone very special."

Putting down his chalk and folding his arms in a smug kind of way, Eddie said, "Hello, Earth to Blade, maybe you can see the light. Dentistry! You can have any days off you want. Work whatever hours you want—no bosses!"

"Well, Eddie, yeah, nice idea—FOR YOU, not me. Good luck with your tooth and thanks for the cookies. Say hi to your mom for me."

And that was that. However, I guess the seed was planted, for that conversation stayed with me for many weeks. I played it back over and over in my mind till one day I decided to seek my buddy out for a little more information.

"I had a feeling you'd be back," Eddie said. "Makes sense, doesn't it? I just happen to have some dental school and dental board applications—and here's some chalk. Have fun."

The rest is history, as they say. At that time, I never could get the hang of the chalk carving. And I must have been the only applicant to dental school who took zero biology courses in college other than the first year required "sleep-thru" Bio 101 class. Since I had been on my way to being the world-famous biochemist, the one who would find the cure to nearly everything, I took mainly chemistry as my science courses. It was quite humorous at the University of West Virginia trying to get the Admissions Officer to understand my goose egg in the biology section of the dental boards. It took a great deal of creative explanation to get him to see the light.

Oh, yes, the University of West Virginia! Let me harken back to that for just a moment ... .

Reflections

West Virginia

I really didn't want to board the plane. But I needed to get to West Virginia for a dental school interview so I had no choice. It was one of those typical Buffalo, New York, late fall days, about 17 degrees with a strong 35 mph or so wind from the northwest. The plane was more than just old. It looked like it had been in the First World War and somehow extricated from mothballs for just this one flight.

"Welcome aboard Lake Central flight 1506 to points south into West Virginia," she bellowed. (It wasn't comforting that a city destination wasn't given.) Our bellower was downright geriatric. She even had on her legs those funny kind of stockings that my Nana used to wear. God save me?

"And where are we going?" she asked. I assumed her question was for me, since I was the only "we" around.

"Morgantown, West Virginia," I replied.

"Excellent" she said, as she chuckled, "Take any seat at all. There should be no overcrowding problem on this flight."

We were due to land in Morgantown that Friday evening around 8:45 p.m. I had reserved a room at the

Morgan Hotel. As I discovered later, it was the only hotel in town. My interview at the university was for 9 a.m. Saturday, with my return flight out at 1 p.m. It would only be a short trip—how much could go wrong?

Actually, there were about six other passengers that night and I think we all enjoyed the excitement of the takeoff. If anyone on board had any affection for amusement parks and other roller coasters, then they would have been in seventh heaven. I threw up and I'm sure I wasn't alone. Even Grandma was seen with one of those cute little bags.

Thanks, Eddie!

After leveling off, our resident caretaker announced that drinks would be served. The unified groan was almost deafening. Only one patron was game and he wanted a beer. However, it seemed that they forgot to put the beer on the plane. Gosh, I wondered what else they had forgotten to put on this tub.

Eventually, I dozed. I guess the jostling about brought me back to my fetal days—the only thing missing were the warmth and security of a mom. The plane was freezing. One large bit of turbulence startled me enough to realize that it was 9:30 p.m. and we were still airborne.

"Hey, Grandma, what's the problem here? Did you forget my stop or was I supposed to ring a bell or something?" I pleaded.

Reflections

"Oh, we have encountered some weather difficulties with snow and wind, and are having a little problem," she answered.

"And what little problem is that, may I ask?"

"Landing."

"Landing?"

"Yes, well, you see, there are blizzard snow conditions throughout most of Pennsylvania and West Virginia, so we are searching for a place to land."

"Searching?"

Have you ever felt your belly button descend deep into your insides and attempt to work itself out the other side? I just made the bathroom in time.

At around 10:15 p.m., I nervously inquired, "And how is our landing situation doing now?"

She responded, "Actually, the captain thought we could land a while ago but there was no chance. And then his second option wasn't good, also. Now, our next shot is coming up in a few minutes. Hopefully, there will be a clean runway."

"And how are we doing for fuel?" I whispered, not wanting to jinx us.

"Oh, I'm sure they've put on plenty."

"Right," my next seat neighbor barked, "just like the beer." It was amazing how we were all bunched together at that point in time. Fast buddies, fast friends, and now we're gonna all die together.

Thanks, Eddie!

Finally, at around 10:45 p.m., our captain announced that he believed that there was a "fairly clean" runway in the next town. We weren't sure what "fairly clean" meant.

The World War I plane did make it down with a good deal of bouncing and sliding. Our group of weary travelers was never so happy to be standing on Mother Earth in the middle of a pitch-black field in the middle of West Virginia in the middle of a bloody blizzard and almost in the middle of the night. We had no idea where we were, but we were alive!

This was just a field. There were no buildings that I could see and the visibility was pretty bad. Grandma told us to wait for a bus, which was ordered and on its way. I asked her where we were in relation to Morgantown, but she didn't know. Nice, so I guess calling a cab wouldn't work.

After one hour of waiting in the storm, a bus did arrive. I glanced at it and then at the conditions of the roads and thought I would be safer on the plane. The bus driver, who looked like he had been getting ready for

bed, told me that in good weather, Morgantown was two hours away. Tonight—who knew? Why was I here? I had already decided never to step foot in West Virginia again, especially if the foot had to step onto an antique aircraft.

Buck was our driver and with his left hand on the sour mash and his right hand on the wheel, I could honestly say the plane *was* safer. Buck's plan was to drop all the passengers at their homes, and naturally, me last in the center of town. The conditions kept getting worse each mile he drove—whiteout snow, high winds, and virtually no visibility. But Buck was intrepid and told us stories of worse conditions in which he drove. He said in West Virginia, this is what you get. Most of the roads we traversed would have been "Out of Order" or closed in most other states. There were huge drop-offs, no guardrails, and no shoulders. Who built these roads anyway?

At approximately 4:30 a.m. Saturday morning, Buck dropped me off in front of Hotel Morgan in downtown Morgantown. This town is not what one would call a booming metropolis. At 9:00 in the evening, there would be no one around. At nearly 5 a.m., you would be hard-pressed to find anything—a cat, an owl, or even a light bulb. I was exhausted and frozen and here I was, standing in front of a totally darkened hotel in the middle of nowhere. Having very little choice, I had to rouse the proprietor, who was not very happy. However, I made the interview and was hitching back to the airport when a couple of coeds stopped to pick me up. Explaining to them that I had a 1:00 flight to catch, they assured me that I would have no problem making it. Snow was everywhere, the sun was out, and the rest of the day was a blur, and no, I never made my flight.

Thanks, Eddie!

The acceptances from dental schools arrived and one of those critical life-defining decisions had to be made. Chemistry or dentistry? Everything pointed to the PhD programs—I had been grooming myself all my life, it seemed, to be some kind of scientist. Plus, some of the offers were very enticing and even financially rewarding. Dental schools gave you nothing.

Looking in a mirror, I saw myself holding in one hand a beaker and in the other a dental mirror, I chose the latter. I don't know why. And not in West Virginia—went to Maryland.

And have never regretted it!

Thanks, Eddie!

Some Dental Ruminations

The Menacing Cotton Roll

There is nothing in dentistry needed more in most procedures than the little white cotton roll.

The next two true stories will show how these little cotton guys have impacted me in my work.

Mrs. Hancock

Mrs. Louise Hancock was the type of patient where everything better go right or else the whole office and possibly everyone in town would know about it. We all know some people like this.

Her appointment was for an impression for a crown and everything went very well. Even the often difficult Mrs. Hancock was thrilled with the appointment and congratulated me and my staff on a somewhat pleasant dental visit.

She was my very last patient before lunch. That day I met a colleague and friend at a local restaurant as we often did. I guess I was about halfway through my grilled chicken sandwich when we all heard a spine-shattering scream emanating from somewhere in that restaurant. I asked my friend to go check it out, since I sort of recognized the voice of the screamer.

Soon enough, he came back with the news I dreaded. He said that some lady patron was having soup for lunch when a renegade white cotton roll plummeted out from under her lip directly into her soup. My friend described the woman in question as being totally in a frenzy and panic-stricken. There was no doubt as to exactly who that lady was.

You have never seen a person leave a restaurant so fast in your life. I truly believe those darn cotton rolls were sent by the devil himself to drive dentists nuts.

Kelly Bishop

Kelly Bishop was a wonderful young librarian in town and was an incredibly easy patient to treat. Our office called her Miss Compliant, as she always did as she was told, including when dealing with some post-bleeding after I removed her wisdom teeth.

She was in the office one day for a routine root canal on an ugly cuspid, or eyetooth. Poor Kelly always had the worst luck with her teeth. The root canal was needed because that tooth had some internal injuries, which I believe, is dentistry's version of an auto-immune disease.

In any case, it's just a single nerve cord and went well. She was appointed to return for the root canal completion in one week.

When Kelly arrived the next week for her follow-up appointment, my assistant Stella noticed a rather unsightly lump under her upper lip. Once seated in the dental chair, Stella calmly lifted the patient's lip and removed the dirtiest, blackest, disgusting, and squishy cotton roll. Usually never at odds for words, Stella was nevertheless dumbfounded. She finally asked Kelly why she had left that cotton roll in her mouth for a whole week.

Kelly's response was quite a shock. Our sweet librarian calmly replied, "Well, Dr. G. left it in there, so it was probably for a very good reason."

Sure thing, Miss Compliant!

Children

Treating children has always been a wonder for me; I have been taught so much by the kids over the years. They see things we don't; they imagine things we cannot. And the vast majority of them are trusting and just fun to be with. I loved playing games with them as we were waiting for the local anesthesia to take hold. Without a doubt, most of the happiest times in my practice had to do with the children and their foibles and quirks.

An interesting two are recorded here.

Robby T.

Robby T. was a dream patient. When he visited me for his first time, he had a continual smile. Nothing seemed to bother Robby. This seven-year-old saw life as his oyster.

Even after being told that he had an incredible amount of dentistry needed for someone his age, he just smiled and urged me to "get to it and fix them."

Our first treatment visit with him was quite long, since he needed stainless steel crowns and a few extractions. Robby smiled through it all and my dental assistants loved him and his attitude. We all laughed and laughed till his treatment that day was done.

Well, after dismissing Robbie and my assistant escorted him back to his mom in the other room, Robbie showed

us a totally different character. With ease, he acted out his con in front of his mother, screaming and yelling that the treatment was horrific and horrible. My assistant is not sure, but she may have seen him wink at her, as this young fellow continued bawling. To forestall any future cons, I asked Robbie's mom to stay in the operatory room and watch the procedure. And she was very happy to do it.

Jimmy W.

Jimmy W. was a very cute eight-year-old boy who absolutely refused to allow me to even look in his mouth. This was surprising, since we had been treating his older brother, Jake, for a few years with no treatment issues.

It took a bit of prodding, but we finally learned from Jimmy the reason for his fear. The eight-year-old confided that Jake had told him that we were very scary, we hurt a lot, and we were probably going to take out all his teeth with disgusting instruments.

Siblings scaring siblings was probably the biggest problem we had with treating children in our practice. What to do?

We came up with a plan which included young Jimmy as a participant. His mother was called and was told of our plan and she agreed.

Mrs. W. brought Jake into the office because we supposedly found some problems with some of Jake's teeth on the x-rays. When he was seated, my assistant put out onto the tray table just in front of Jake's eyes the scariest instruments she could find in my cabinets.

Of course, Jake started to sweat a little and asked my assistant what those tools were for. Stella then told the twelve-year-old that she was sure that I was going to use them on some of his teeth. She also indelicately brandished a large needle in front of Jake.

By this time, Jake was panicking and ready to bolt, but Jimmy, who had been hiding behind a wall, burst into the room and yelled just one word at his older brother, "Gotcha, Jake!"

The 99-Year-Old

Mrs. Rosaria Piarria marched into my office one day and demanded to see the dentist. It's amazing how much a 99-year-old can get by just demanding it. My receptionist seated her and scooted out of the operatory as fast as her feet could take her. This was one scary lady!

I guess I had been in practice about fifteen years and thought I had seen everything. But I was mistaken.

When I entered the room to see this nearly six-foot woman sitting in my chair with stockings rolled up to her knees just like my nana used to, I knew this would be no ordinary patient.

"May I help you, Mrs. Piarria?" I asked.

"And sure, you are dentista?"

"Yes, I plead guilty, I am. How may I be of service?"

"And stop with the small talk," she barked. "I need some teeth."

I have had my head chewed off before, but it was eerie having my deceased grandmother doing it again. And this woman was tough. You could immediately tell. All dressed in black, hair done up in a bun, black shawl over her shoulders. Yes, very tough!

"Would you rather be called Mrs. Piarria or Rosaria, which was my nana's name?" I quickly responded.

"Eh, you fixa my teeth, you call me anything you want. Are you Italian?" she demanded.

"Well, yes, one hundred percent Sicilian," Hoping this would back her down.

"Ha, you don't scare me. Just fixa my teeth. I cannot chew with these dentures. You fix and everything will be OK. Now, get started."

I did as I was told and checked the condition of her mouth, which was fabulous, except she had no natural teeth, only a set of dentures. And they fit as well as could be expected with the amount of shrinkage in the lower jaw that a 99-year-old woman would have. I told her that, and she started flailing her arms demanding I do something.

"Cannot eat bread anymore," she screamed. "There must be some new-fangled way to make teeth work."

"Well, Rosaria, we do place implants today and these small fixtures help to hold the dentures in place. However, with your advanced age and the surgery and healing required, I'm not sure … "

Cutting me off, she yelled, "How much for these plants?" And, when I reluctantly replied, she screamed, "You gotta be kidding me—way too much money. Let me outta da chair, I gotta go home and think about it."

And with that she was gone. Phew! Sure as hell didn't want to start treating her—even if there had been something I could do.

My luck ran out one whole year later when once again Rosaria barged into the office like a cyclone and demanded to see the dentist. "I thought about it and I want dose pegs," she cried. She was even scarier at a hundred. There was no stopping this woman. She made me make an appointment with my oral surgeon for a consultation on the "pegs." I was sure he would just tell her they couldn't be done on someone her age and that would be that. Back then I did not do the surgery.

"Hell, Harold, I hear you saw Mrs. Piarria earlier today." I was calling my favorite oral surgeon back. "Yes," he said. "Rosaria is an amazing woman. We're scheduled next week to place two lower implants in the cuspid area and she'd very much like you to be present during surgery. And so would I."

"Harold, her age! Will there be osseointegration?" "Who knows," was his answer. "The studies only go to age 85. We may be setting new standards. And, are we to refuse Rosaria?" I guess not. And, certainly Harold was also quite amazing. Getting away with using her first name during her first appointment!

The incredible woman came through surgery without a hitch. Her jawbone looked awfully good. But it would be the healing, which would make all the difference. With implants, bone has to attach to the titanium under the gum and become one with the implant.

This process, called osseointegration, is the key part of the whole procedure. And this is the part where advanced age is a severe detriment. Once integration takes place we would be able to hang teeth or a denture off the implants. The normal waiting time for the mandible is three months. But with Rosaria, we waited four. I wanted to wait longer, but in the old Chicago vernacular, "she weren't getting any younger."

Harold proceeded to do the second stage surgery, which means he first exposes the implants and places a temporary abutment sticking out of the fixtures awaiting healing. So far, so good. And I was there every step of the way. Rosaria was Rosaria—tough, demanding, and intrepid.

Three weeks later, enough healing had taken place for me to place the permanent abutments and start with my impressions. We were working very hard and fast to make this work. By tapping on the implants, we can get a good indication of osseointegration by the sound. In her

case, one sounded fabulous and one a little less so, but I was still cautiously optimistic. Usually, when implants fail, it happens right away. We were three weeks into it after second stage and around five months after initial placement.

The day came finally when we were to give Rosaria her new implant-borne denture. She came in. No black on. Red dress. No rolled-up stockings. Hair done. Son in the waiting room.

I put in the appliance—screwing them in as carefully as I could. It was when I got to the second implant that I heard the awful suction sound. The whole implant was turning—no osseointegration. Sort of like screwing into a molly and the whole molly is turning. Shock and despair went through me. My assistant knew, of course. I had to face Rosaria and tell her. This would be heart-breaking and difficult.

But, no it was not. Rosaria could tell from my face. I guess my tears were a dead give-away.

She looked at me and before I could talk, she said, "Eh, dentista, vene ca (come here)." whereupon, I came up to her, she put her arms around me and gave me the warmest hug I've ever received in my life. "I've had eleven children," she said, "and twenty-eight grandchildren, and

seven great-grandchildren, I've had some die, most lived. I have had lots of disappointment in my life, as well as lots of good things. You and dottore Harold are some of the good things. Don't be sad, you tried hard."

Thank you, Rosaria, and peace be with you wherever you are.

Lisa Marie

"Jackie, who is my noon consult? Have I seen the patient before? And is that a joke—you have a fifteen-year-old girl who wants a consult regarding extraction of all her teeth?" I'm sure my face showed extreme bewilderment, as I asked my receptionist these questions.

"I'm not sure, Dr. G. A woman called to make an appointment for her niece, Lisa Marie Coudes, for a consultation for full-mouth extractions. The aunt, Gloria Hapsheal, said that this will be difficult, so give enough time for this visit. That's why you have two hours scheduled, but I'm as curious about it as you."

Noon arrived approximately when it normally does and Mrs. Hapsheal was led into my private office.

"Thank you so much for seeing us, especially on such short notice. I'm pretty much at my wits end with my niece, Lisa, and finally agreed to bring her to a dentist to have all her teeth pulled out."

"You are welcome, Mrs. Hapsheal."

"Please call me Gloria,"

"Ok, Gloria, let's start at the beginning and give me some background about this whole situation." I was so curious I was almost bursting at the seams.

"Well, yes, okay. Lisa Marie is my sister's child. My sister and her husband live in West Virginia and have had a rough time. My brother-in-law drank and couldn't keep a job so my sister had to go to work to help support both Lisa and her little brother. The domestic situation there was awful, and nine months ago, Lisa ran away. She was just fifteen years old. I'm sure it must have been very difficult for her—a drunk for a father, somewhat abusive, but I'm not sure of that, and an absent mother.

Well, anyway, my niece arrived at my doorstep eight months ago. She had been travelling on her own, poor dear, for one whole month. God, when I think of all that could have happened to that child … well, Herb and I took her in. She's been with us since."

"Lisa is enrolled in high school, but hardly ever goes. She never, as in NEVER, smiles. She has no friends. So on and so on.

I'm sure you get the picture. We've tried everything—the school psychologist, a private psychiatrist. She's now on some medication, which has helped a little, but all we get out of her is she wants her teeth out. So here we are. Please help us."

Whew. What a story. Poor Lisa and certainly poor Mr. and Mrs. Hapsheal.

"Have you seen her teeth and the reason for her request?" I asked.

"No, we haven't. It's not like we haven't tried. She eats in her room and, like I said, never smiles. She talks with her mouth closed and always always has a hand in front of her mouth. We've even tried sneaking into her room when she's sleeping and prying her lips apart to see, but it's dark and we don't want to alarm her and have her run off from us like she did from my sister."

"Does her mother know she is with you and your husband? I want to find out more information about who would be responsible for this child."

"Oh yes, and she's delighted. She even sent us a signed form allowing us to be her guardians so we can have her medical needs taken care of. Now, Dr. G., if you are concerned about your fee, let me just ease that by saying, Herb and I were never blessed with children so we would spend whatever is necessary to take care of our unfortunate Lisa."

"Well, Gloria, I was asking primarily for responsibility, but I see genuine love and concern in your face so I just hope that I can help her. And I'm sure that doesn't mean removing her teeth. Now I think it is time to see her."

We walked into one of my rooms where Lisa had been placed and my eyes fell upon the most beautiful young lady I had ever seen in my life. She was standing leaning against the wall. She was radiant. Perfectly proportioned physique, high cheekbones, terrific round dark blue eyes, auburn hair clipped very short, a nose the greatest plastic surgeon would die for, strong chin and skin like cream, Lisa stood there scowling with lips tightly together.

"Hello, Lisa Marie, my name is Dr. G.—your aunt has brought you here for me to look at your teeth to see if we can do anything for you."

After a few seconds of sizing me up, all she said was "You can take them out. That's all," all the while covering her mouth with her perfectly proportioned hand.

"Well, Lisa, would you kindly sit in the dental chair for me. It will be impossible for me to do anything with you standing in the corner."

I could see the dilemma she faced. Lisa would have to give up some control, especially difficult, to a stranger. I guess the softness of my expression caused her to slowly move towards the chair and sit down.

"Now, Lisa, would you like your aunt to be present or not?" I cautiously asked.

"Yeah, she can stay, but not where she can see my mouth. Only you see."

"That's OK with me," I responded and asked Gloria to stand by the entryway looking away from the child's face.

I switched the operating light on and the youngster really jumped out of her skin.

"Lisa, it's just a light. My eyes aren't as good as yours so I need a strong light to see."

"You're just gonna pull them out, right, and give me some false teeth, right?" She sounded very determined.

"Well, Lisa, I need to look at them first to determine what we are gonna do." She became agitated and sat straight up. "So we need to take measurements for the new teeth we will give you." Calming down, she put her head back on the headrest. After much pleading from me and more internal anguish on her part than I'll ever know, Lisa Marie finally with her beautiful eyes closed opened her mouth.

The incongruity of this situation immediately overwhelmed me. Here, she was the most beautiful young female with the most misshaped dark and crowded dentition I had ever seen. No wonder Lisa wouldn't smile. And if one doesn't smile, one can't be happy. Researchers have found without question, just the act of smiling brings happiness and health. To go through years without it would be like going without food or love.

Two of her teeth were fractured in half. One central incisor was tilted 180 degrees so that the inside portion of the tooth was facing out. Her two cuspids (or eye teeth) were high up not having enough room to come into place. This gave a strong "fiend" impression. The level of her gums as they approach her teeth was all over the map. Some high, some low. But as bad as the shape and location of her teeth and gums were, the color of these unfortunate teeth was even worse. Some were brown with white spots, some were opaque white with brown spots. It looked like a severe case of dental fluorosis—too much fluoride ingestion during the formation of the teeth. There was no doubt that whatever water she was drinking in West Virginia had far too much fluoride in it.

I checked her teeth for decay, but there was none. Her teeth were as hard as could be. Her gums were very red and irritated, both from the crowding and the lack of proper homecare. I'm not sure I would have cleaned them if they looked like that either.

What a cruel twist of fate—Beauty and the Beast all in the same person. What could I do? I was thinking as fast as I could.

"Lisa, how did these two teeth get broken?" I asked. Her response was unexpected. "I hit them with a rock trying to move them, but they stayed, just broke. So when will you get them out? Auntie says you could do it today. That's why I came."

"Lisa, let me show you some pictures first." And I handed her some photographs of patients with beautiful smiles who were born that way.

"Yeah, I want that," she lit up immediately.

"Ok, Lisa, let me tell you now that their teeth were very jumbled—not as bad as yours—but not very pretty. This patient was thirteen years old when we started and she is now eighteen with this smile. We did not take out her teeth—we straightened them with braces, took a few of the bad ones out, and then covered them with either caps or laminates and this is how it looks."

Her interest was definitely piqued, but she was still pretty determined to have them all out.

"My mom has false teeth and they look fine. These teeth I have are no good. Please just take them out."

"Lisa, dentures will make you look old before your time." And I went through all the other reasons not to have dentures, but to no avail. This was getting very tough and I didn't want to lose her. I felt drastic measures were needed so I did something I had never done before. Time to call the bluff and pray.

"Stella," I called to my assistant, "please get ready for surgery." I winked at Gloria so she knew. My assistant stacked the tray with the most gruesome instruments I own. This tray, which is normally covered and away from the patient, was no more than a foot from her face, Lisa's eyes were getting bigger and bigger and a little teary. I then brandished the largest needle I had right in front of her face and did my best to make it look as painful as possible.

"What, what is that for?" my poor patient cried.

"Well, Lisa, you don't expect me to take out all your teeth without numbing them. Let's see, you have twenty-eight teeth, so I'll have to inject you with this about fifteen times to properly pull all of them. Are you ready?"

This is when she broke down—sobbing uncontrollably. Stella was hugging her; Gloria was holding her hands and I was moved to tears myself. All those years of torment—family life and physical deformity—all coming out in torrents. I let her cry. And she did.

When Lisa finally calmed down, I sat next to her in my private office and like a father, told her that her aunt and uncle loved her. They wanted the best for her. We wanted the best for her. It would take a great deal of effort on all our parts, but the end result would be worth it. I would need to make preliminary impressions for study; she would have to see an orthodontist, an oral surgeon, a periodontist and then me. It could take four years to complete. I pleaded my case and Lisa was receptive.

The case did in fact, take five years. She had six teeth extracted with laughing gas. Her orthodontics were done after I placed some normal tooth-colored temporaries on the most discolored of her teeth. Periodontal surgery was performed to give her gum line the proper contours and levels. And a combination of full coverage crowns and porcelain laminates were fabricated where necessary.

Lisa Marie started coming out of her shell almost immediately after the discolorations were covered and the braces were on. After all, about half of her high school had braces.

Mr. and Mrs. Hapsheal spread more love on her than many natural parents. Gloria has stated over and over how Lisa's coming to them was an act of God. They weren't meant to have an infant, only a high schooler.

The day when the final dentistry was placed and the pictures taken is one that stands out in my mind as if it has lights on it. We all cried and hugged and laughed. Lisa is now in graduate school. She wants to be a psychologist so she can help troubled youngsters. And she'll make a damned good one.

When things go bad, when dentistry becomes too hard for me to continue, as it does some days, I just remember why I am doing this. And there is no greater reason than Lisa Marie Coudes.

Veronica

If you have ever questioned the mind/body connection, the following true story about Veronica Blake might be of interest.

Veronica was the great aunt of a good friend and patient. His name was Eddie and a real prince of a man—ex-military, handyman who could fix nearly anything, old car collector and James Dean impersonator. Eddie loved going to those car shows to not only show off his old Chevys and Fords, but to revel in the 50's and 60's music which he loved. Eddie unfortunately passed away early, but before he died, he introduced me to his aunt, Veronica.

Veronica Blake was a well-to-do older woman who always was impeccably dressed. She became my patient and somewhere along the line, she protracted a particularly debilitating type of Parkinson's. Treating Veronica in a dental setting was extremely difficult and bordered on impossible.

One day, I saw that there was a consultation scheduled with a woman named Delores, who apparently was Veronica's daughter. During the consult what struck me most was the absolute love that this woman had for her mother. Getting right to the point, she told me that Veronica loved being treated by me and my staff. Delores then confided in me how her mom felt about life and other things. She stated that her mother could absolutely handle almost anything—including her Parkinson's disease, which, at that time, was terrible, and she could even handle dying. What she would not be able to handle well and would be horrified about was the prospect of losing her teeth. I told Dolores that that is far from uncommon.

Delores and I both discussed the incredible dilemma we faced. Her mom had been totally unable to stop shaking for the last few months. That fact made cleaning her teeth, even with her aide's help, virtually impossible. Doing dentistry on that type of moving target was also virtually impossible. During our consultation, I assured this loving daughter that I would do everything in my power to save Veronica's teeth.

Remember those first attempts at treating her were disasters. All of us in the office loved Veronica and wanted so very badly to treat her successfully. However, we always ended the visit with all of us crying.

Then, one visit, and it might have been my last attempt, I tried something different. After her aide, who always brought her in a wheelchair managed to help her into my dental chair. I whispered to Veronica that I needed her help to save her teeth. Her aide was shaking her head apparently thinking imploring her would not work. Undaunted, I begged Veronica to give me just two hours of her being still. With tears in both my eyes and hers I heard her say to me, "I will try Dr. G., I will really, really try."

That is precisely when the miracle occurred. Veronica relaxed her head on the dental pillow, closed her eyes, and after taking a few large breaths, she totally stopped shaking. We were all shocked, including her live-in aide, who just could not believe it and remarked that this was the first time in many months that she was still.

After yelling to my staff to cancel the rest of my morning appointments, we worked feverishly to save as many of her teeth as we could. After three hours, Veronica looked at me and my assistant and asked if she had been good. Once again we all broke down crying—this time happily. We had just experienced an incredible miracle of her mind controlling her body.

To this day, Veronica remains one of the absolute top experiences of my life.

Change

Finally I take the huge
step off the treadmill of
my life
placed there by my
second grade teacher

She was a nun after all
and might have had
divine inspiration

So how could I be
so foolish

Why have I waited
so long to get off
the treadmill.

I guess we all believe
we will crash and burn
if we move out of character.

Change is always frustrating

But I learned about
change
in high school

It even has its own symbol

I'm now a much older man
and just beginning to
understand.

Remnants

There are always clues
to past behavior
remnants left
like
crumbs on a plate

Actions gone bad
actions gone good
demarcation of a
soul
gone this way
and that

A twice lived
life
remains to be
discovered
and
judged

Only to be
irritated by
the incessant
wail of

recalculating

Damian Galbo

When

When did it become
acceptable
to maim and kill?

Man's ability to
perform horrific acts
is legendary

The ease with which
some people—
justify evil
sometimes leaves
me breathless

I guess it is now
okay
to just kill a child
because you refuse
to take care of him

I guess it is now
okay
to remove healthy organs
from a mentally disturbed
individual because they
don't like who they are

We have come so far
in the last thirty years
soaring and soaring
and lower and lower
it'll get very
hot soon

Damian Galbo

Sensations

Some things are hard
to experience

I used to wonder sometimes
how it felt
to drown
to suffocate

I'm beginning to understand the
sensations
of each

Upstairs and Down - Measuring What Has Been Lost

The first memory he had of his name being spoken came on his third birthday. There were the requisite friends and songs. It wasn't till a few years later, however, that he realized the importance of his name. He wasn't a Timmy or a Billy. He was Nino. After his grandfather they said. The boy could not understand how or why he was named after someone he neither knew nor saw. Indeed, this elder Nino had never even been held in much esteem by the family.

Young boys can be cruel, and inevitably, fun was made of his name. How much this affected his disposition will never be known. But he was sure it played a part.

He had always wanted a dog. Not a cat. Robbie from down the street had a dog. Dogs were hungry and he felt this was how he would secretly discard his unwanted dinner. Robbie said he had never been caught. The boy, however, was sure he would have been caught.

In his home, cooking odors were omnipresent, and they were so horrible as to suffocate him. Grandma was responsible; she was in the house all day basically raising the children. She used an old-fashioned pressure cooker which was on from morning till night.

Nearly all the food products in the house went into that machine, cooked for hours, and came out soft and inedible. He believed their grandmother could only serve food which had been killed. The smell permeated the whole apartment. It was pungent and it was awful.

Teased outside, asphixiating inside, the boy needed to find a safe place. He discovered the basement and the whole world opened up to him.

The basement was extremely large, the whole length of the house. Except for one room, it was unfinished, dark, and ominous. Three small rooms—no more than large closets really—had wall-to-ceiling shelves on three walls. At the very rear of the basement there was a huge kitchen which, interestingly, was sunlit from the backyard. This had been possible via a cutout in the earth so that windows could be placed and sunlight could enter.

The boy spent hours in the little rooms, traveling. A tiny, low wattage light bulb gave a bit of illumination. When on, eerily strange shadows were cast making the room just frightening enough to be exciting. Sitting on a small low bench, he would close his eyes and listen to the silence being spoken.

It was here that he voyaged with Robinson Crusoe, Jules Verne, and others. He could hear waves crashing, the roar of a locomotive, and the quiet of the submarine. He could be a cowboy waiting for the Indians, or an Indian waiting for the cowboys. Limited only by his imagination, he stretched as far as he was able.

The boy felt safer and freer in this mysterious and clandestine space than anywhere else in the upstairs world.

It was again about on his third birthday that he started to wear glasses. Back when the boy was growing up, glasses did not increase his popularity with the other children. He had a strange name, wore spectacles, and went to a different school—the nun's school. He tried his best to fit in, but never really succeeded.

Although he found refuge in the dimmest corners of the basement, it was in the windowed, bright room where he really flourished. There he would sit near the window with the sun on his face completely free from the upstairs world. He had some stamps, and he loved them. His favorites were from some South American countries, and an island name Ceylon. They were so colorful, almost musical. He easily visualized being where the stamp depicted. The stamp book which someone bought for him went unused. The boy felt strongly that the stamps should never be glued down in a book. He left the book upstairs.

After college he tried to find his stamps, but could not. He was able to remember what many looked like, but not

Ceylon. Going to a map he discovered the island was no longer called Ceylon. Maybe that's why.

He was sent to the nun's school two bus lines away. He was not unhappy about it. The sisters favored the youngster, filled his head with dazzling predictions of greatness, and even became surrogate to him. The boy believed these prognostications, and started to revel in their optimism, and to gain much needed self-confidence.

However, it soon became clear to the youngster that he had no extraordinary intellect, only some unique gifts. He seemed to have the ability to ask the right questions in class which made him seem smarter than he was. And on tests he knew exactly what the teachers desired for answers. This was all intuitive, not intellectual. It was like in college when playing basketball. He always knew where the rebound would come off the rim. It has to do with physics, geometry, spin rates, angles, torque, and speed. The boy never used any of these disciplines; he just knew and so it was in grade school—he told them what he knew they wanted to hear. And he flourished.

Instinctively recognizing how the sisters yearned for conformity, he delivered. Later, at his all boys private high school where the brothers also demanded conformity, he once again used his instincts to succeed. He found the dead language, Latin, fascinating. He was excited by the

Reflections

patterns of words from Latin roots to English. The boy was completely taken with linguistics. To this day he wishes he could be more understanding and less judgmental of language failures seen and heard every day. It is difficult for him. He blames the nuns and brothers, but he sings their praises for it as well.

The young boy's pride and joy was his vast marble collection, maybe three or four hundred strong. All sizes, shapes, and colors—cat's eyes, iridescents, translucents, and opaques. In the large room downstairs he would place a white towel on the table and proceed placing his magic stones—writing words, drawing pictures. This was pure joy for the boy.

Much later, after college, he returned to the basement to find them. They were gone.

But he lost much more than his marbles by going to college.

The college years depicted the ultimate upstairs world to him. Those years and his graduate years were exceedingly cruel. The boy lost so very much participating in group think. Each new math problem solved brought another more complicated one to decipher. Like a hamster running constantly on its wheel, he could not get off. In these centers of higher learning which claimed to spawn independent thought, he discovered that, yes, one may attempt to engage in that direction, but it must be kept within certain guidelines. Without fail, parameters were set. Even in philosophy, the professors were more concerned about what other "philosophers" thought than what the boy thought.

Those years went by fairly quickly and the parchments were given to him. These were forever evidence to him of all he had lost—his freedom. He was now on a path (with guardrails) to "be" someone. His religion—he found intellectualizing a Creator quite daunting. His imagination—he could no longer imagine a voyage to the center of the earth. Most of all, the boy lost the ease with which he was able to live, dream, and think outside boundaries.

Civilization's Demise

We are on the precipice today. A calamity greater than any earthquake is occurring now and will certainly continue till humans go the way of the dinosaurs. The end of civilization as we have known it is upon us.

Many possible causes can be put forth as reasons for this self-destruction. There is the depletion of the ozone layer, the acceptance and ease of procuring and taking drugs, the serious fall of the family, the proliferation of items of mass destruction and the ease of attaining them, maybe the growth of antibiotic-resistant super bugs, the destruction of our forests and natural resources, and many, many others.

Without doubt, all of the above are extraordinarily serious and are having dire and regrettable consequences. However, our demise will occur way before all of the above pull down the final curtain. It is happening today and growing louder and stronger each and every day. And it is taking place everywhere on our planet.

The epidemic of Silicon Valley's handheld technology is destroying the very fabric of what it means to be human.

Twenty years ago, people held hands. Today they hold a device. Twenty years ago, they took a walk, heard the

Damian Galbo

song of the birds, saw the beauty in the trees, and smelled the fragrance in the air. Today, during that walk, our senses are blind due to our brains being occupied using our machines. Twenty years ago, individuals in restaurants, cars, and other places, spoke to each other. Now, that happens rarely. If a person were to leave their device in the car or somewhere by mistake, one or both parties would have to immediately rectify that and position their gizmo right on the table next to their food and certainly next to their hand.

Cars do not start right away anymore when the light turns green due to the addicted having to complete their text or tweet. Years ago people knew how to spell, knew grammar and sentence structure. No more. The age of abbreviations and LOLs, etc. and the age of spell-check is upon us. And God help us. It hasn't taken long to shrink our brains.

Interviews or discussions with young professionals can be quite uncomfortable. Their social skills without their device in hand are woefully lacking. A walk with children was joy and a learning experience. Today, grandchildren cannot wait to return to the house and their devices.

A recent study showed some teenagers would commit suicide if their handheld machines were taken from them for any length of time. And they freely admitted this. They also admitted their inability to put their devices down or turn them off. The average time they could tolerate without their machines being on and in their hands was ridiculously low.

How much longer do we have as sentient human beings who have forgotten how to be sentient? It used to be fun at a social gathering to discuss who may have written a particular book or who composed a certain symphony. No more. Today, someone at the table looks it up on their phone and spoils the fun.

There is very little thought going on today; there's hardly any deduction, and ridiculously poor writing.

The threshold has been crossed; humans cannot go back. Technology is ruling the world and quietly turning people into addicts and robots. We will surely disappear soon. AI is here now!

In our quest for speed and immediate communication and gratification we are successfully and quietly causing our own demise.

Some Sobering Thoughts

Over fifty years ago a history professor in college asked the question of us: to name the three most dangerous current happenings, which could possibly spell the end of civilization as we know it. This individual was certainly one of my favorite and most erudite teachers.

We in class came up with many possibilities—for example: communism, nuclear war, dictatorships, the permissive drug culture, bigotry and many others. I was thinking recently that I would like to perform that exercise today. I certainly have plenty of choices, but I've narrowed my most dangerous things to three.

My list, for what it's worth is as follows:

1) LIBERALISM

A complete definition of this belief system is difficult due to the large number of tentacles which reach in many directions. One would be social re-engineering, which includes gender confusion and history rewriting. Another would be the concept of political correctness and the categorization of people not as individuals but as a member of a group with only a modicum of commonality. One tentacle could be the absolute right to murder innocent, unborn children and the right to squelch the speech of dissidents to them. Others include the belief that everyone should be allowed to enter our country, maybe our homes, also. They believe the doctrine of the mother spigot and dependency. But mostly, it is the group think mentality which is central to their thesis, dangerously limiting individuals to have the freedom to dissent and to be individuals.

I place this evil dogma first in my list due to its insidious persuasiveness. This doctrine is being taught, both subtly and blatantly, in most of our school systems from grade school to graduate school. Our children with their eager and fertile minds are continuously being led down the path to this progressive culture. Could it be that our education system has been hijacked by teachers and professors who discovered this destructive philosophy during the permissive and wild 60's and 70's?

Their simplistic group think view of nearly everything causes its proponents to absolutely stand for no difference of opinion and allows them to attempt to eradicate any heterodoxy. This insidious credo is almost like a viral disease. It purports to save and cherish our fellow man, but does not allow for him to become self-reliant and good on his own.

2) INTERNET AND SOCIAL MEDIA DEPENDENCE

This is certainly not difficult to define and until the last ten years or so this was a non-existent problem. However, the present addiction to technology with its instant and constant communication is causing grave mental and physical concern for the current and following generations. Not to be linked causes anxiety. It will only get worse. Try to take a cell phone away from a teenager.

These devices have basically eradicated individual and original thinking. The machine does it all.

I can envision a time when robots will perform most of our tasks. Like muscles which atrophy from disuse, so in this way will go our brains. There will be no more art, no more literature, no more humanity. This is a very scary future.

And, yes, there will be just a few select people in control of these devices—the ultimate dictatorship.

3) EXTREME FANATICISM

Whether religious or political, being on the extremes of either causes incredible hatred and sorrow.

Religious fanaticism has been with us for centuries, even as long as recorded history, and has not lessened in intensity. The prejudice it fosters is beyond dangerous, because its proponents really believe they are doing God's will.

On the political side, the far right and the far left have no room for others in the middle. As with religion, this churning of intolerance is justified by the group and allows them to destroy and crush, by whatever means possible, their opponents and even the world as we know it.

Thoughts on Life

A chemical equation is clear: mix Part A with Part B and there will be a resulting formulation. Can we narrow life down to a simple formula?" Let's attempt to do so.

Part A: Noise, confusion, tension, anger, bustle

Part B: Calm, understanding, silence, solemnity, love

If we then mix Part A with Part B, we get life. And our will gives us the ability to choose. But if we choose only from Part B and call this our own view of life, can we truly say that we have experienced life? If we select only what brings us comfort, the resulting formulation will be very skewed. When we attempt to escape by choosing the safety of stagnation, boundaries are never pushed. Growth is never realized.

It is only in stretching almost beyond our limits, that is, adding Part A in our formula that we have even a modicum of chance to grow. The great enigma of living is that it is only by "letting go" and mixing all parts of the formula that we are able to capture life's true essence. But "letting go" does not mean running in place. It denotes acceptance and contentment, while selecting all of life.

So I postulate that we must mix all of Part A with all of Part B to be truly human.

Love

Many years ago a teacher once called me obtuse and since I had already taken geometry, I had some idea what he was attempting to say. It was clear to me then and even much clearer to me today that he was only pushing me to be more creative, imaginative.

Over the years I oftentimes would think of either being obtuse or creative. Or being sad or being joyful. None of these words allow us to touch them. A box I can touch. A toothbrush I can touch. Happiness, loneliness, etc. cannot be touched. But these touchless ideas in our life are probably the most important elements we have. They are feelings and it is in these feelings that our very personhood is defined. And that personhood can change in a moment's notice.

Dictionaries have so many "feelings" and "affections" listed that the mind boggles at just reading some. None can be touched, none can be captured. Humanity, cowardice, courage, pride, arrogance and the list goes on and on.

Obviously, there are some which are considered better than others: kindness is a better feeling than hatred, patience, better than impatience. If I were to choose just one feeling that I would like to have and others see in me—that would be love. All else pales in comparison.

Damian Galbo

Letters to My Brother

Following are letters
from two long-lost
brothers estranged for
many years. Personal
matters have been removed,
so the letters
can be included here.

Reflections

May 6, 2001

My dear Harry,

It was beyond great hearing from you, brother, after all these years. How many years has it been for us? Fifteen, twenty? I know it was just a birthday card (I'm amazed you still remembered)—absolutely love that you sent it.

Are you still living in Canada? I hope we can now begin to communicate on some kind of regular schedule. After all, we are brothers only a few years apart from each other.

I will certainly respect your request in the card to only send snail mail to each other. I agree with your disdain for all things internet.

A little about me quickly—living in Naples, Florida. As much as you used to hate the heat, brother, I hate the cold.

I anxiously await your next conversation. It's wonderful for us to reconnect.

Your loving brother, Richard

Oct. 10, 2001

Dear Harry,

I'm surprised that I haven't heard a word from you. As you are probably aware, this country was attacked by some radical Islamists and thousands of Americans and others were killed in the World Trade Center disaster. I am still shaking from it having watched it mostly unfold on television.

Harry, I know you detested this country years ago but even you should be appalled at what happened on Sept. 11th.

Please let me know if you are living under a rock and possibly don't know the news.

Richard

Nov. 19, 2001

Harry,

Thanks for your recent letter and your condolences. I sincerely hope they are truly heartfelt. It seems to me that I have somehow been violated and probably will need a good deal of time to get over it.

I assume you are pretty safe up there in northern Canada. Sadly, your brother will get back to you when I can.

Richard

Damian Galbo

Jan. 20, 2003

Harry

Time has surely flown. It seems like only yesterday that the tragedy hit New York. However, two years have gone by and I am finally able to collect my thoughts about it. By the way, two close friends of mine were lost in that attack.

I'd love to hear from you with news of what you are doing and what transpired in your life since 1968. I tried calling, but there's no known number for you.

Rich

April 3, 2008

Dear Harry,

    I was hoping you would respond to my last letter, but five years have passed and nary a word from you. I checked the internet and I believe you are still alive and, I hope, well.

    I cannot believe that our disagreement thirty-some odd years ago is still festering. When you left for Canada that horrible day in 1968 I just assumed you would return and certainly not stay estranged all these years. I did my duty at that time in Nam. You did what you felt you must. I understood your objection to the war and your marching and protesting about it. Since that seems like two lifetimes ago, please let us reconnect.

    I believe you should be happy since I believe there will be a liberal black president elected soon. Not being a fan of his since he has absolutely no record of ever accomplishing anything, I, however, will give him some time to prove me wrong.

    I'll give it about six to twelve months to see if he can accomplish anything and fulfill the wishes of the large white liberals who see him as some kind of Savior figure.

    Please respond if you can, if only to say you are OK.

Richard

Damian Galbo

Oct. 12, 2010

Dear brother,

Your very short missive to me recently was very welcome. I am happy you are keeping well, but would love more info on what you are doing and if you ever plan on making a visit.

As far as this new President goes, I believe he is an abject failure. Actually, he is doing exactly what he proposed to do. He wants to somehow change this country according to his mentors, all quite radical. He has instilled "race" in nearly every facet of our living. Sure, this country had many who were biased, but this guy sees it everywhere.

Remember when I was playing basketball for my college and I was the only white on the team? Well, none of us then saw us as being different from one another. I didn't see black. I didn't see white. Now this guy in the White House has made everyone conscious of color. And the worst part is he has been doing nothing for the black community to bring them out of the ghettos.

It's sad because so many people think he's wonderful because he has great diction and poise. But I believe he is an empty suit and will be very harmful to the U.S.

I'll keep you posted as time marches on.

Rich

Feb. 4, 2013

Hi Harry,

Well "empty suit" has just won a second term in the White House. I have a sneaky feeling that you are happy about that. We always were quite opposite in our thinking.

I feel driven to sit down and tell you some things about this fellow.

While he was developing his speaking skills he wrote some books explaining to the "masses" just who he is and what he is about. Many who read his books could not help being sympathetic to him and actually became followers and even revered him.

His education and demeanor have made him a darling with the "intellectuals" and academics. And his severe left political stance has him as the "heartthrob" of the media. As I stated to you a few years ago when he won for the first time I was wary and alarmed from the beginning and it has played out like I thought it would.

The massive programs for redistribution of power and wealth are greater than any I have ever seen before. The power is being sucked from the "private sector" and given wholeheartedly to the "public sector." The wealth is obviously being redistributed from those who have earned it to those who "had they been given a chance, might have earned it." Modern Day Robin Hoodism. And, Harry, I bet you probably agree with all of this. After all, you are living in a socialist country.

Sorry, brother, for the long rant.

Yours, Richard

May 6, 2016

Hello Harry,

Thank you so very much for your fairly long letter giving me some idea what you've been doing all these years. I always knew you were interested and very knowledgeable in mathematics, but I never realized you were teaching math and even writing math and engineering books. Bravo to you, dear brother!

I am sorry to hear that you had been dealing with some serious health issues. As the mathematician in the family you, of all people, know that time waits for no one and takes no prisoners.

My health for the last few years has been fluctuating between good and bad. Recently, it has been good and the simple fact that we are communicating again has lifted my spirits enormously.

It looks like we may be in for a surprise in the next election down here. It could be quite entertaining and I'll be sure to keep you well informed.

Richard

Damian Galbo

May 19, 2016

Hi Harry,

    I am shocked and super excited about receiving one of your books. It came by FedEx yesterday. From the date in the jacket it looks like it might be your latest. And a signed version! What a treat! The title, "Complex Differentiations with New Thoughts on Cauchy-Riemann Equations" is enough to give me a headache. I am going to just place it on my cocktail table so when guests arrive they could just think that I am a little bit smart.

    Love, Richard

Reflections

May 2, 2017

Hi Brother,

Well, we have a businessman in the White House. That is some change. Donald Trump is a New York real estate developer and television personality. What I can tell so far, and there hasn't been a lot of time for evaluation, is that he is brash, unafraid, crass, arrogant—in other words, a typical New Yorker. (I can say that because I am a New Yorker - hopefully, not as arrogant.)

Early on it looks like it will be hard for him to govern—he is being attacked already from all sides. And the non-stop nonsense of Russian meddling has finally gotten me to turn off the news.

On a nonpolitical note, I was wondering what your favorite course was in undergrad college? A group of friends just had this discussion and I thought I would ask you. My favorite course was organic chemistry—no math needed on that course—just a great deal of logic. My most difficult course in my chemistry curriculum (I was a chem major) was Physical Chemistry and the understanding of the movement of fluids. Bernoulli's principle is still my favorite equation even though for years I never fully understood it. I wonder what your favorite equation is. If you have time jot a bit back to me.

Thanks,
Rich

Damian Galbo

Nov. 15, 2017

Dear Harry,

Thanks for your response to my two questions. I'm sure you are quite busy working so I appreciate your short letter. Your favorite course was one taken in high school, Advanced Calculus. You say that that was the course that brought math into, as you say, your frontal lobe. And your favorite equation being Newton's Law of Gravity, $F = G \times M \times m \div d^2$ was also surprising. Even I understood that equation.

Thank you for answering.

Harry, I plan on sending you a Christmas card. Is the address at Sturgeon Falls, Ontario, still good? It seems that your last letter had a different return address. Someday, we shall have to discuss how we both came to our present domiciles.

Richard

Reflections

April 6, 2019

Dear Harry,

It's amazing how time flies. Our last communication was almost two years ago. I know I've been busy down here in Naples. Just got finished building a home down here. You would hate it because the houses are so close to each other. If you need some sugar or milk you just have to stick your hand out one of your side windows.

Remember how growing up our house was almost five acres and totally secluded? I'm getting used to the fact of no land here but I doubt you would last any time at all.

The country seems to be thriving and these last few years, our president seems to be working hard and it is paying off. However, he is still the most hated man in America.

For some years now I have been writing blogs and now have many thousands of followers. I will include in this letter one of my recent blogs having to do with President Trump. Please feel free to criticize or evaluate in any way.

Richard

The Huge and Unrelenting Chasm in America

The pundits say it's Trump's fault. It is not. He's the target, not the cause or the fault. He is, however, the most hated man in America.

What Donald Trump did to earn this notoriety was to simply win an election. How dare he??!! Yes, he is crude and has many faults. However, he is not putting people in ovens, he is committing no criminal acts during his presidency. What he did was realize that there was a large part of this country which could not care less about political correctness, about gender politics, about climate change. What these people cared about was jobs, putting food on their table, lower taxes, less government, better health care, and bringing back God into our culture.

So this man runs on this agenda and, even with all his many faults, beats the high tax, low growth, big government left wing opponent. The liberal intelligentsia, the liberal media and the entrenched politicians of both parties could not actually believe it occurred, especially by this less than genteel man. To make themselves feel better and to offer the possibility of removing this man from office, they came up with the Russian theory. He could have only won with the help of the Russians.

The relentless characterization of Mr. Trump by the media, elites, and educators as a cross between Joseph Stalin and Charles Manson or between Mussolini and de Sade has finally borne fruit with their convincing millions of people in this country to hate this man with a passion unseen before in our history. So many people have been indoctrinated to hate everything about this person that he probably can no longer govern. It used to be that people differed on policy decisions, but still respected each other.

When I ask some of the "haters" to mention something egregious that Mr. Trump has done (other than policy decisions) their response usually is "he tweets, he offends peoples, he's an ego-maniac, he's crude, he's had a dubious past," etc. Can the fact that he gets his message out by tweeting be the cause of such intense hatred, many actually calling for him to be removed or even worse?

Whatever President Trump does, he is criticized daily and mercilessly. He visits our troops and he is castigated. If the previous president had done the same thing, he would be praised. The left wing elite hate him so much and want him to fail so badly that they do not even care what happens to the country as long as this man fails. This is exactly what the Federal Reserve is doing by raising interest rates when there is not a hint of inflation. Trillions have been lost due to their willingness to beat back this excellent Trump economy.

I used to blame the "indoctrinators," the CNN's and *New York Times* of the world. I don't any longer. They are only doing what they have been programmed to do. Now I blame the "indoctrinatees," the "haters" who believe the nonsense they hear and read. These "haters" should look in the mirror and ask themselves if they have indeed been brainwashed to hate. The large chasm in this country, the rift presently caused by these "haters" can never be healed unless some objective introspection takes place.

No I do not blame Mr. Trump for all of this.

Reflections

June 19, 2019

Harold,

It seems that a scourge has hit our country and the world. The virus, called Covid-19, has been let out, presumably by China and is causing havoc here. Is it the same up there in Canada?

People are homebound, must wear masks, and the elderly or others with some medical issues are simply dying.

There are many thoughts as to the origin of this plague but the soundest seems to be the Chinese releasing this to the world due to our President's tough policies toward that country.

I had even begun to consider a trip up north to see you but that is impossible now; travel is pretty much out of the question.

They are working on a vaccine for Covid but as far as I'm concerned I shall be very wary about putting some novel substance into my body until it is tested for many years.

Please let me know if this virus is impacting you in any way. Since you mentioned in a previous letter some medical issues with which you are dealing I hope you are staying put and protecting yourself. As for me, I am not going anywhere.

Rich

Damian Galbo

Aug 2, 2020

Dear Harry,

I'm very happy that you have been able to dodge the virus. I guess staying where you are in a very unpopulated area is protecting you.

Unfortunately, I have not been that lucky. I contracted the virus about eight weeks ago and can really say it was an experience. The worst part was the demon sore throat. They call it razor throat—so very painful to swallow—much worse than strep.

I took the medicine they gave me for three days then had to stop. The meds were worse than the Covid issues. I am happy to report that other than some olfactory issues and lack of saliva issues, I am fine. I'm told that it might take over a year for my salivary glands to start working again.

I am sure you know by now that President Trump lost the election last year. I'm having a difficult time figuring out how an incapable man who has been in politics for 40 years and has done nothing could have defeated a very good president. I guess when everyone is against you, you cannot defeat those odds. The election integrity is being seriously questioned since it is nearly impossible for this winner to have gotten over 80 million votes.

I guess we are stuck with him and his left-leaning handlers. I am not sure this country will be able to survive the next four years. You have a left-wing dude as prime minister in Canada. I'll keep my opinion of him to myself, but I'd love to hear yours.

Stay well, brother,

Richard

Dec. 18, 2022

Hello again, Harry,

Another year is almost in the books. I have fared decently down here in Florida and as long as I can read, play chess, bike and golf, then I am quite satisfied.

Our economy here in the states is lousy—very high inflation. I'm starting to worry if I'll have enough to last thru my retirement. This high tax, big government, big spending administration is doing us no favors. Also, they have destroyed the energy sector with their fascination with green nonsense and electric vehicles. I wonder where the batteries will be trashed when they all die. Has Biden's stupid policies hurt your economy since much of your economy is strongly energy related?

Included in this note is another of my blogs, one which was written about six years ago. I hope you will read it. Your positive statements about the blog I sent were very much appreciated.

Love, Rich

It's All About Control

So, how are the masses controlled by the elite power brokers today if the "Wrath of God" doesn't work anymore? Since the new left has virtually eliminated the Creator and/or religion these days, how can the general population be controlled? For centuries the means of keeping people in line was the fear of God.

The neo-fascist left has needed a new game plan for today, and they have certainly found one. The fear they bring now is from the demise of the planet due to the nebulous "climate change." And this "change" is being orchestrated and nurtured by what we humans are doing, by living.

Computers have been programmed to spew out dire consequences to us unless major changes are made. And the power brokers will certainly tell us what we can and cannot do. The "new" ersatz "scientists" are using their bogus statistics and studies to prove their point. The numbers they use are tailor made to make their point and to frighten the average person. Their lies are not checked—their torch carriers are the left wing media. If they say we only have a few polar bears left, that becomes gospel. (As a point of information, the polar bear numbers are way up.)

As long as a few—as little as two—generations can be led to believe in their bogus hypothesis, then these generations can be led to do just about anything the power seekers demand. How the general populace eats, travels, and lives becomes so important to the health of the planet that this fear can be overwhelming to these people. This can be seen to be working as well or even better than the "fear of God."

This whole climate fiasco is a very intelligent and well-thought-out method to seize control of the masses. When ten-year-olds are striking at school from fear of dying in a few years, you know then that the power and control brokers have indeed won.

Dec. 14, 2023

Dear Harold,

    I had a strong feeling that you would not agree with my last letter's remarks and my last blog regarding Climate Control. You have not changed from who you were in the 60's. That doesn't matter. I still love you.

    With that being said, please be on the lookout for a Christmas gift, which I sent to you last week using FedEx.

    I would love some comments from you.

    And Happy Christmas to you, Harry.

    Richard

Jan. 10, 2024

Hi, Harry,

Quite a quick letter back from you—it seems our reconnection is going well. You are most welcome for the gift. I published "Reaching Inward" last year after I got my act together and refreshed and collected some of my writings, both prose and poetry, from the last forty years. Your kind words about the book are appreciated much more than you know.

You, Harry, were always the math genius. My interest seemed to always lay in language and writing. It seems our destiny in some small way is now fulfilled.

Have a good winter, brother, and hopefully the snow and wind up there will be to your liking.

Richard

Reflections

April 12, 2024

Hello again, Harry,

Lots of stuff happening down here in the states. We have our previous President involved in many circus trials so he won't be able to campaign again for the White House. The senile congenital serial liar now occupying the White House seems to be orchestrating, probably his henchmen, the whole fiasco. No one knows where it will lead, but I believe Mr. Trump's popularity is greater than ever and those sham trials are hurting the democrats more than Trump.

Also, it is impossible not to be aware of the foolishness of the morally adrift children protesting for a terrorist group on many college campuses. Antisemitism is very prevalent once again in the world and that is certainly true here. The low IQ students out there demanding Israel not defend itself from a horrific act of war from Hamas is mind-boggling. Those morons have no idea of the history of the region and all that Israel, the UN, and a few Arabic states have done for the Gaza residents for the last fifteen or so years. They probably had never heard of Arafat.

I know, Harry, you were a hippie once and maybe still are one, but I cannot imagine you could be calling for the annihilation of the Jews. Hopefully, all this garbage will be confined to the poison ivy schools, which continue to be the centers for Marxism, perversion, and anti-semitism. Stay well, my brother, and stay above the fray.

Richard

May 10, 2024

Harry

That was a quick response from you. Maybe, and hopefully, you didn't want me to include you as one of those intolerant wokesters who sell utopia, then deliver dystopia, nihilism, chaos, and totalitarianism.

You very logical explanation of those protestors having a right to their opinion was well thought out. I'm glad you added the proviso that they should not cause any harm to any group.

Harry, I have to admit that I fear for all of us. I think we are as close to World War III as we have been in over fifty years. We were both teenagers when the Bay of Pigs took place. I remember both of us figuring that world war was imminent. However, gladly, we were wrong. Today, however, with wars going on in Eastern Europe and in the Mideast, I fear that the clowns governing here have no clue what to do. And not only that, they basically hand-fed a nuclear bomb to Iran by giving them massive amounts of money.

We haven't mentioned religion at all in our many letters. I still am a believer and hope you can believe in some presence greater than us. I pray every night for this world, which, at times, seems ready to implode.

Stay well, my good brother,

Yours truly, Richard

Damian Galbo

Love Lost

His mind was cluttered with
last week's problems
still unsolved

Getting to this point
of having no time
or maybe
no inclination to
start up his brain
was terribly
unsettling

That organ
once hailed as a
machine to be admired
easily solving the
most complex of
problems
lying dormant now

Reflections

He has finally realized
at this very late time
in the game
that the catalyst
for his massive
machine
was thru the heart
and that organ
must be fed

Damian Galbo

Mirage

                A mirage?

                Perhaps…

For over a year
two hearts
molded together
as one

but…
…
…

falling in love is
a very dangerous game

and then…

the sound, the roar
heard first
a river

blistering water
raging, hurtling
over the rocks
in a tempest of anger
frantic to arrive
at its destination
a precipice, a small cliff…
   once over
finally exhausted
resting in a large pool
of stillness

Water rushing to
find peace
masquerading as calm

and then…

Stealthily the fog
arrives
quietly, quietly
attempting to

Damian Galbo

obliterate any sense
of sight
of truth
obliterating even the
perception of truth
of peace
of love

one is
left with a surreal
taste of elusiveness
of reality
blurred
…
…

And what of me?
I guess
I can handle this
by believing the whole episode
to be an
illusion

Perhaps it was!

Danger?

They warned me that
She was out of my league
beating the drum that she is
a heartbreak for sure
bellowing to me that
you know nothing about women
like her
she will eat you whole and
spit you out.

But, but
never seeing her accompanied
and looking so very fetching

Disregarding all the warnings
A voicemail was sent
and incredibly a response
was received
certainly cryptic

Been eyeing you for a while
so it is quite lovely that you
finally noticed me

Damian Galbo

Without a doubt, my new friend,
I believe you will certainly
Be a very tasty
little morsel

Maybe It Is Time

For decades now, conservatives have been attempting to legislate correct or moral behavior. Unfortunately, this has been met with mixed results. Maybe now is the time to give up this folly.

The left, especially the women on the left, are extremely ardent supporters of choice. They are so very impassioned about that one issue that it seems to be the only concern for which they care. Many are almost militaristic in their defense of this issue. The fact that there are myriad methods of pregnancy prevention, both before and after insemination, seems to have zero impact on their thinking.

Now is the time for the right, the conservatives, to stop all the anti-choice legislation and lawsuits, and to just allow the people who want to murder their babies to do so.

Indeed, if they are so intent, as many of them are, to maim physically healthy, but mentally deranged children, maybe the conservatives should not stand in their way. Let murderers be murderers, let maimers be maimers, and just assume that at some point judgment will arrive for them. It has happened in the past (see Sodom and Gomorrah) and history has a tendency to repeat itself.

If conservatives ever desire to win another major election so they can fulfill their agenda to make government smaller, to make taxes lower, to deal with the insane deficit, to stop the wars, to fix the border chaos, etc., etc. then they should immediately stop trying to legislate morality. The people on the left have little interest in morality and are so insanely passionate about choice that the right cannot hope to win their battle at the election box.

Raison d'être

The space between
the treadmill of life
and the stillness
of death
is where I currently
reside

A destination as
enigmatic as that
of the narwhal

I am teeming
with uncertainty
and longing to
know the raison d'etre
before complete darkness
closes in

Waiting, waiting

I wait for the bolt
to hit me
to explain my purpose

Damian Galbo

Yet, when it came
I was totally
unprepared

trembling and in shock
I accepted the gift

My destiny, my gift
the discovery of love
and the joy
of sharing it
as often
as I can

My Wish for Myself

The struggle to maintain inner peace, calm, quiet and safety in the midst of the cacophony of routine life is one of the greatest challenges we must all face.

If it were easy, there would be absolutely no value—the greater the difficulty, the larger the reward.

We can retract from the world, or we can embrace it with a clear and uncluttered heart. It is imperative that we measure our success each day by the number of quiet and contented heartbeats we have in relation to those which are troubled.

We are given oxygen to breathe; it is what each of us does with those breaths that really matters.

My wish for myself is that I breathe deeply, sing loudly, love strongly, and dance unabashedly.

Milton Keynes UK
Ingram Content Group UK Ltd.
UKHW031353011224
451755UK00004B/358

9 781614 939757